Art Is The Thing Nobody Asked You To Do

Babak Ganjei

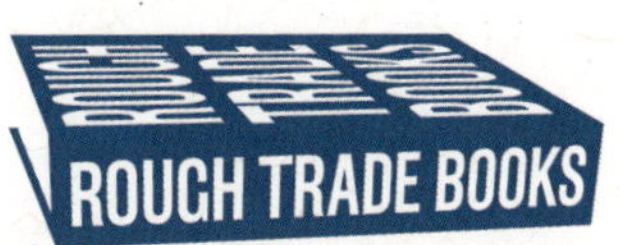

INTRODUCTION

Off the bat I need to tell you I really struggled to write this pamphlet. I'd said I'd write an Art Manifesto, but then realised I lacked the required levels of authority. So I started to write a sort of exploration on art, but each attempt started to feel disingenuous after a paragraph or so. I used some words I didn't know the meaning of. I dug up a Foucault quote. Three quarters of the way through essays I would find myself disagreeing with my own carefully thought out arguments. Nina at Rough Trade Books told me to write what I know. This resulted in three weeks of not writing anything at all.

It's hard to know what you know.

It's because I want this to be good. If you are at Art School, I want you to pull this out and quote it to your tutor, and I want your tutor, a respected practising artist, to grab it from you, thumb through it and announce to the class that their eyes have been opened. I want them to give you the rest of the day off.

The pressure to achieve such dizzying intellectual feats has led to all sorts of diversionary tactics. I hoovered. I started running long distances. I perfected a recipe for tomato soup. The key is anchovy paste as a salt substitute. To be honest, it could double up as a Puttanesca sauce.

Here ends your first master class.

ART SCHOOL

Art school is where I learnt to smoke.[1]

She's Going To Leave Me (2017)

Taken from the series *IKEA Business Workout* (2014-2018). Every trip to IKEA I would take photos pretending to work on the computers in each showroom, but over time, a greater narrative started to develop. The photos were instantly documented on Instagram. Photo by Sophia Wimpenny

1 It cost £27,000

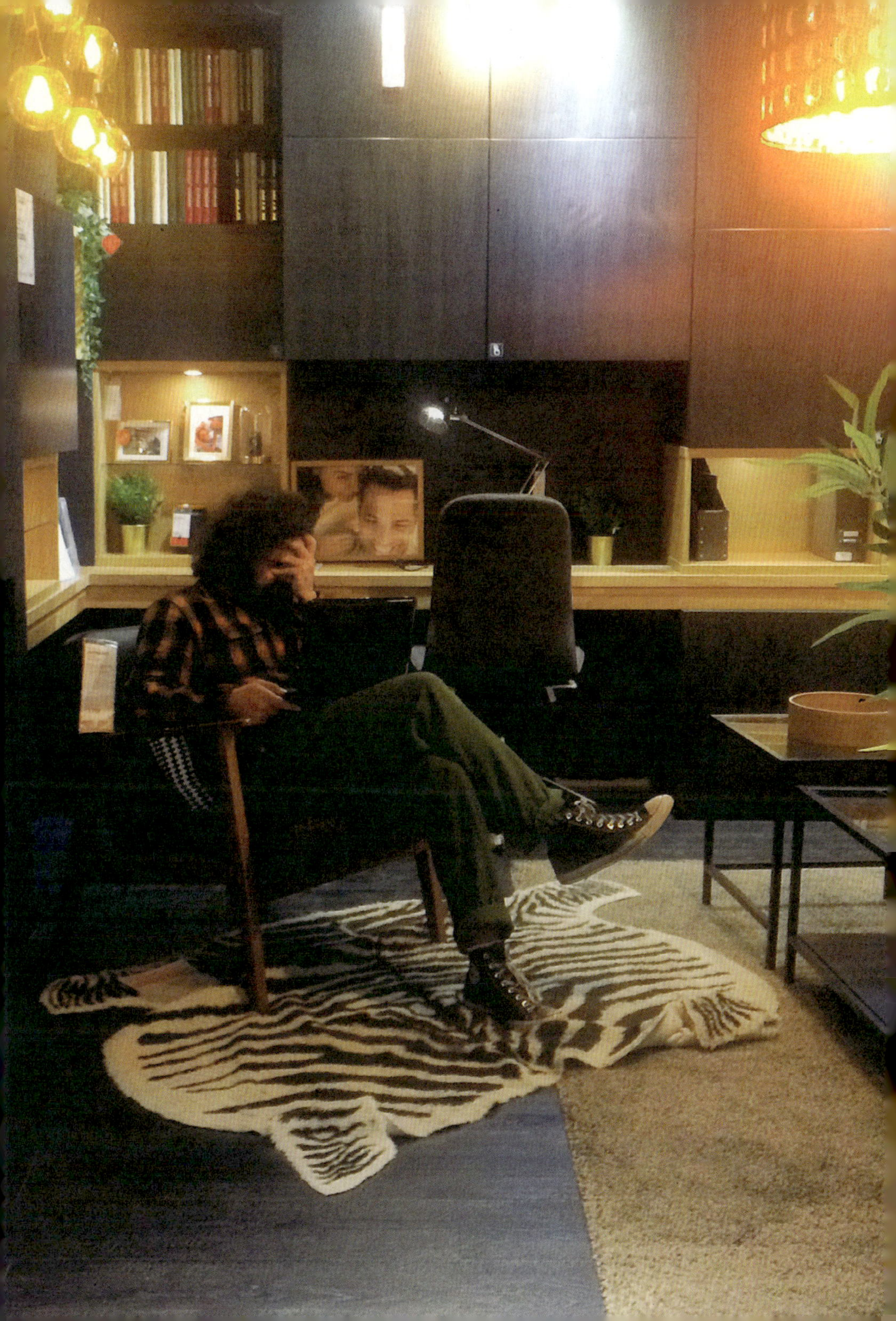

BE FROM NOWHERE

A couple of years ago, I was hit with a sudden realisation. I'd always thought the person who bullied me at school was a girl. But when I thought about it, it happened in the boys' toilets. And he was called Dominic. These facts only really registered at a Tesco Express self-serve kiosk 32 years later. Unbeknownst to those behind me in the queue, I had just added psychological baggage to my basket of potato waffles and Jelly Tots.

My parents moved to the UK from Iran in 1977, and I was born the following year. Farsi was spoken at home, so English became a second language I strung together via the TV and song lyrics printed in Smash Hits magazine. I didn't speak at all at school until I was seven. In the interim, I relied on my Smurfs sweatshirt to do the talking.

At school, en route to the toilet, Dominic would be stood, sandwiched between a sink and a hand dryer, much like Lyle in *Infinite Jest*.[2] Dominic's bullying was mild, aside from one occasion where he poked me with an index finger. To be honest, looking back, he could have been trying to invite me to his birthday party.

I should clarify that these early years were not as depressing as they might sound. I was busy. I was busy making marks on any surface going. The underside of my dad's desk was covered in layer upon layer of scrawl. Who knows what I was trying to say? It didn't matter. Mark-making was a silent, violent language, and I was a master of it. Hieroglyphics meet Cy Twombly. A coded language that when eventually deciphered would probably read 'please buy me Castle Greyskull'. Self-expression, after all, can be shallow.

Many of you will come from beautiful places which offer stability and comfort. My experience is that

of a person who never felt like they belonged in any place.
Someone who at the age of 42 can be reminded that they are
not immediately perceived to belong to the only country they
hold a passport for. I have white friends here in the UK who get
defensive when I talk about this sense of not belonging. They also
grew up feeling misunderstood and different. However, walking
into a country pub in Norfolk, they don't feel like they are wearing
a sombrero. But this is not about racial abuse. As I've gotten older,
I've come to notice that it is often me strapping on the sombrero
as I walk through the door of the pub.

For an artist, it turns out to be useful to be from nowhere.
I'd even recommend it. To not belong to a town or city or country.
And though it's considerate to check in with them from time to
time, to not really belong to your parents, especially as they may
not share your sense of displacement.

Early on in the Brexit debates somewhere around 2016
I was feeling hurt, angry and betrayed that the discourse on
nationalism was gathering pace. My parents were far less emotional
about the whole thing. They are a couple who left their country
and made a new home in another one. They were never under
any illusion about their status in the UK. Their calm acceptance
of the whole situation got me so riled up, I kicked a chair. It
was totally out of character. But I did hold the top of the chair
with both hands so it didn't actually fly across the room and
hurt anyone.

An artist needs to be free. Displacement is a shortcut
to this and brings with it a desire to communicate and seek
connections with others, be it as court jester or reporter. You
might even find these roles easier as an outsider. An interpreter
of a language you don't entirely own.

Basically, never get too comfortable. I say this for purely
selfish reasons, as deep down I envy anyone with a sense
of confidence and entitlement. I live each day with a 'thanks
for having me' approach, like I'm on an after-school playdate.
My identity doesn't come from a sense of place; it's a buffet
of the culture I consumed growing up. Smash Hits pop lyrics,

Back To The Future,[3] canned laughter, a bit of Bruce Willis, Transformers, He-Man, Kurt Cobain's suicide, and Dominic in the toilets.

When I got home and unpacked my two items of shopping, I realised why I might have randomly remembered Dominic so many years on. One day after school, my mother suddenly appeared in the classroom doorway with the teacher. It was very strange to see her enter this alien world of mine. My teacher sat down beside me and pulled out a large bag of Jelly Tots. A big bag, like one you would take to the cinema. My teacher said if I would say 'hello' I could have the bag. It seemed crazy to say hello—it was the end of the day!!! I should be saying 'goodbye'. But I didn't want to get into semantics. I said 'hello' and collected my sweets.

Everybody has their price.

[3] I left the cinema feeling like I totally understood romance. Let's forget this was romance between a mother and son. The eighties were a strange time for morals in mainstream cinema. Or it could have just been Michael J. Fox films. In his 1987 film *The Secret of My Success*, he almost has an affair with a woman who later turns out to be his aunt. I went to see this with my aunt.

You Are Alone (2017)
Canvas flag left on Margate beach.

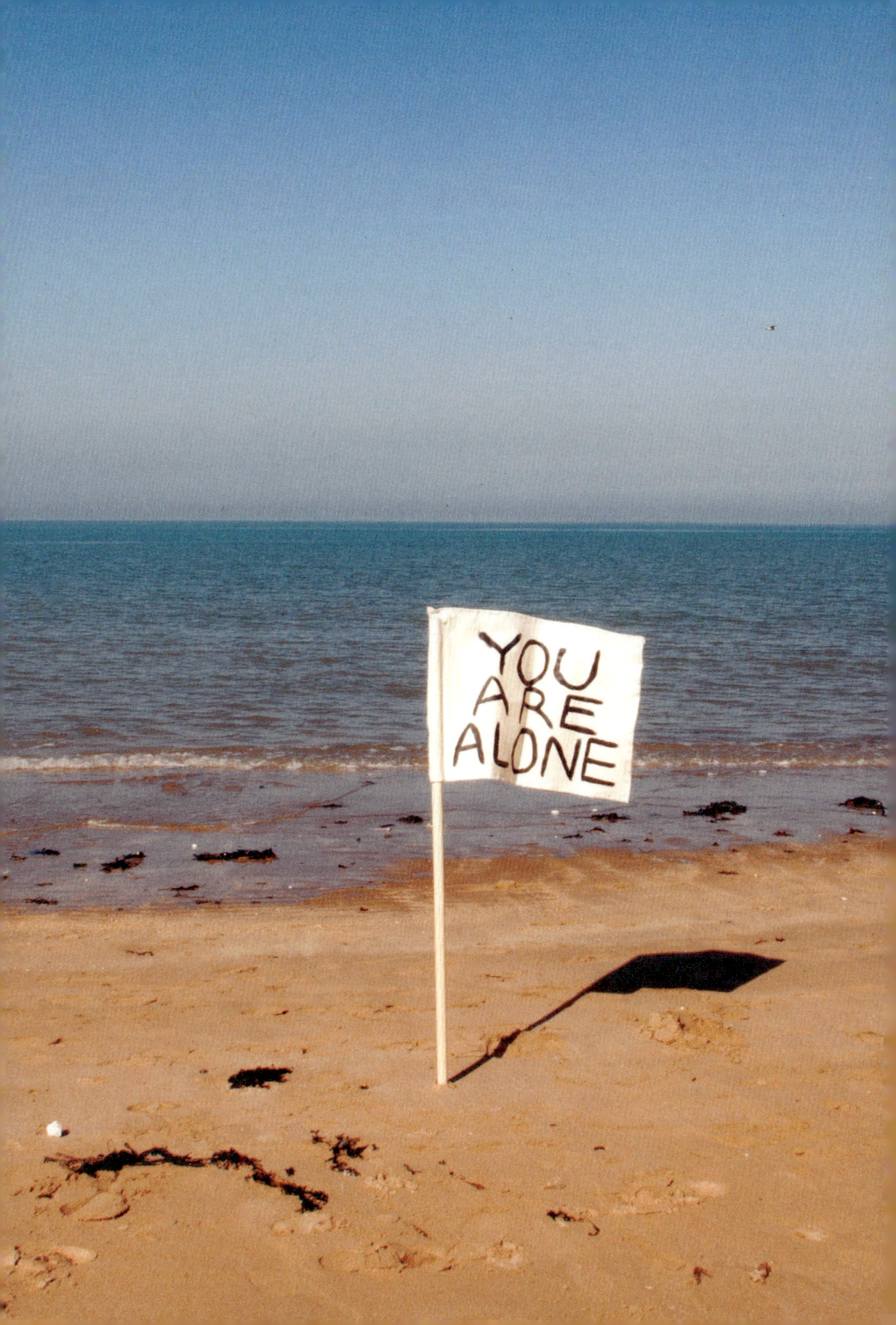

YOU
ARE
ALONE

TECHNOLOGY

I'm queueing up to use one of the eight computers in the library
at Central Saint Martins. It might be the only time I've used a
college computer. It's a late 90s IBM with a green screen, because
it is the late 90s. I'm only waiting because my girlfriend has set me
up an email address, and I have promised to write her one of these
'emails'. I live with my girlfriend, and it's more than likely I will see
her before she reads it, which adds a curious complication: what
do you write to somebody you speak to every day? It's like sending
a secret.

This moment happens during a very brief period of time
when new technology works alongside the existing means of
doing things. On introduction, unless you're a space engineer,
it's a frivolous novelty. The shopping lists and bill reminders and
daily chores could be done in the real world. This was something
unnecessary. An esoteric, dreamlike space where your inner
monologue is verbalised.

Walking out of the library, I was adamant: this thing
would never take off.

I was late to the mobile phone. My first one was a hand-me-down
from my younger brother: a blue Motorola. I had previously
been given a pager for my birthday from a friend who I can only
presume thought I had aspirations of becoming a doctor. The
pager involved people paying to call a middle man to ask them
to send me a message to call them back. I would then go to find
a payphone (an Edwardian structure covered in sex flyers).
It was expensive and time-consuming for all parties. To my
knowledge, I was the only art student with a secretary holding
my calls. As with technology, alcohol and hot dogs, I resisted
having a mobile for as long as I could because I have an addictive

From: Babak Ganjei
Sent: 17 SEPT 1998 13:27
To: ███████████████████
███████████████████
Subject: FIRST EMAIL

Hey!

This is weird, like speaking in the third person or something. I never had a pen pal or anything like that at school. I always imagined if I was writing something like this it would be to somebody in Africa that I would never meet. He or she would then send me a picture of a chicken or some other exotic animal on their doorstep to highlight the physical and environmental distance between us.
I am also not a good Typer. I am doing this all with one index finger so it leaves me more time than I like to think about what I am saying and makes me conscious to know that I don't know what that is.
I Guess I will see you later but you will know that already, as it has probably happened, but then I guess it's going to happen again so this is still relevant until it isn't.
How do I sign this off? Do I put my name on the end? It seems a bit formal. Suddenly I feel this distance that didn't exist. I'm in my head. Welcome to my head.

Regards
Mr Ganjei

personality, and once I've given in, I'm all in. I was okay without one.

When you don't have a mobile, you have nothing and it's fine. You make plans and you show up and if someone is late, you wait. One day, I arranged to meet a friend in Soho to watch a retrospective of Vitto Acconci films. You don't need to know that part, but it's true. I was running late because now I had a mobile and could afford to be. I could just let them know. We were digital people who could locate each other next to the cat calendars in a bookshop via a satellite orbiting the Earth.

But then the phone dies and there is a bus diversion and you are thirty minutes late, and you have fallen into the abyss. I waited at the arranged meeting point in Borders like a lost child. There was nothing that could be done. I'd never felt that powerless, and despised the hold the device suddenly had over me.

Obviously, as soon as I got it recharged, I resumed my game of Snake.

I don't know what happened to my friend, as I have not seen him since. I have forgotten his name. If you ever happen to bump into somebody looking for me, tell them to get in touch at babakganjei@hotmail.com, and I'll do my best to explain.

2005

The other day, I was logged into PayPal, and I noticed it said I had joined in 2005!!! Sixteen years on PayPal! I still have no idea what it is. I used to think it was just a very open program for laundering money, but now I have an accountant, and he says it isn't. I would love to be transported back to 2005 and work out why I even needed to join PayPal, since I never had any money.

The internet has blurred all days, months and years, and now time is meaningless. Decades aren't defined like they were in the 20th century. There is so much going on, so much culture swimming around everywhere. Things move so quickly. An idea can be realised and posted on Instagram in 37 seconds (other speeds are also achievable). Everything is everywhere, and for that reason, we are nowhere.

Today I have completely lost sight of what it is I am doing. Lying in the dark, *Top Chef* beaming from a tablet balancing on a selection of books that will never be used for anything other than supporting tablets. I scroll through Instagram on the phone, sending goodnight messages to strangers at 3AM. The show is over for one more night. It's twenty-three years since I dismissed the internet as a needless frivolity, and I am trapped inside it as an avatar, a jester, activist, consumer... artist. However much you might want the validation a gallery brings, you no longer need it. You can find your own audience. You're free to create your own trap, and the opening hours are 24/7.

SELL - OUT

I'm struggling to write slogans for a new surfwear company. I'm always surprised when people ask me to do things like this. 'We love your attitude and wit. We think it works really well with our message. Can you just tone down the negativity and sarcasm?' (For context, they have approached me off the back of T-shirts I've been selling with 'Dead Inside' emblazoned across the chest.)

This would have all been fine if the company was aimed at depressed surfers weighed down by existential dread, but the 'Ride the Wave' images they have emailed me suggest they aren't so niche. I've never touched a surfboard. I can't think of a circumstance when I might need to. My idea of an extreme sport is riding an elevator to the top floor.

The paradox of a company employing an 'independent' artist to fulfil a brief is that once they have paid to secure their spirit, it is no longer independent.

SPAM EMAILS FOR SALE

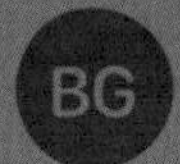 **Babak Ganjei**   26/04/2021
To: babakganjei@hotmail.com >

Spam Email

Good tidings

Dear beauty it has been so long since we have
never met. My name is Princess . Do you believe
like me that destiny is like a flightless bird that
never took off? I believe it too. It was confirmed
when my mentor and cleaner Richard Fettucini
exploded in an elevator.
It is a mystery you cannot make up. I have so much
bleach and a proposal that you can refuse. I miss
your beautiful eyes of which there are two?

Please reply to my proposition I am angry with you
email me on badenemy91@aol.co.uk

Spam Email (2021)
I started selling bespoke Spam emails
on my website for £12.99. At the time
of writing I have sold one to somebody
in Canada.

In the pit of my stomach, I know this isn't right. I've written 'Breathe the Wave' on a piece of paper, and I hate myself. I mean, I don't know what it means. It's shit. I'm pretending to be somebody I'm not.

I'm pretty sure they didn't realise the levels of torment they had brought upon me by offering me paying work. Why did I feel like a sell-out? More importantly, why did the idea of being a sell-out matter to me still, in my forties with a child to support? I realised that any time I get asked to do a job there's a voice in my head asking... 'what would Kurt think of this?' Then I have to remind myself I'm now 15 years older than Kurt was when he took his life. I'm 21 years older than the kid who wrote the words to the songs that gave me the confidence to be myself, and the truth is that we don't know what Kurt would do now, or what he may have become. And as much as this is a tribute, I'm also a little bit angry at him for not having left me any answers.

Kurt Cobain was my first and most influential curator. At thirteen, Nirvana became the gateway to a creative underworld I never knew existed. It was 1991, and my family had left the multi-cultural melting pot that is London for Bournemouth, hoping to make a name for ourselves as the local non-whites.

I was now an outsider, and I needed backup. My instincts told me I had to shift into darker territories. I remember knocking on my parents' bedroom door to warn my mum I was contemplating buying the Guns N' Roses' *Use Your Illusion* albums with the gravitas of someone admitting to having killed a man. My mum didn't understand what a Guns N' Roses was.

The albums were okay. Definitely edgier than my Johnny Hates Jazz tape. The swear words, the attitude, the lit cigarettes dangling dangerously amidst a mop of hair which probably had some sort of flammable product in it. But there was still a disconnect. It wasn't real. They were characters, like a boy band or The A-Team. The band was a show. It was theatre, and I don't mean to dismiss theatre, but I was looking for a space to inhabit, not to simply be an observer. I was looking to get lost.

I still remember the day I opened the *Nevermind* CD case in WH Smith's in Boscombe on a rainy after-school afternoon in full uniform. The image of three blurred men with the middle guy giving me the finger. I kinda didn't like it. It was uglier and scarier than the leggings and hairspray being offered up previously. I shut that case quickly as if it would summon spirits if left open any longer and walked away feeling like I'd seen something I wasn't supposed to. Within that case, an untapped world was spinning, and despite the contempt it seemed to express for me, I was being drawn in.

Suffice to say that within a month, I was so fully on board with the Nirvana anti-corporate agenda that I had gone back to Our Price and returned my Guns N' Roses CDs. I wanted nothing to do with them. Nirvana led to other bands like Sonic Youth, who in turn introduced me to artists like Raymond Pettibon, Mike Kelly and Dan Graham.

The value placed on the authentic was a much different thing in the 90s. It was a time where, on occasion, *Twin Peaks* would be one of only four things on the TV. There may have been less culture available, but when it broke through to the mainstream, it really wasn't going to go ignored. People paid attention to the charts. If a band from the underground made it onto *Top Of The Pops*, it meant something. *Nevermind* knocked Michael Jackson's *Dangerous* off the billboard chart.

In the 90s, there were still clear lines between the mainstream and the underdog. Now we live in seemingly more democratic times. The tools to make art in all mediums are more readily available to a greater number of people than ever before. Yet it seems like it's still a privileged elite running the show.

Democracy of production only seems to have diluted the impact of production. Subcultures all exist in their own space, and you can ignore them freely. Nobody needs to be exposed to anything they didn't choose to see. And when most of this work is housed under the umbrella of Instagram or Facebook, the ideas of independence and authenticity are less easily defined.

I'm aware of the irony here—Nirvana broke the mainstream on Geffen Records, a major label. The unfortunate dichotomy of art as a career is that an artist's principles generally lend themselves to socialism—they are of the people looking to connect with the people—but to succeed as an artist, it's individualism that is celebrated, and that thrives under capitalism. Communist Art is either regime advertising or craft.

The difference is that in the 90s the battle was a choice. Nirvana's ambition led them to sign on the dotted line, and subsequently agonise over having done so. Today, it's a post-ironic mess. We are all free to create as individuals, and social media and other online tools have stripped away some of the hierarchies, but at the end of the day, we are working for free as content providers for technology conglomerates who we have to concede won't pay their fair share of taxes.

So with that in mind, why is the fear of being a sell-out still so strong? We (I) should feel liberated knowing that the fight is futile.

Sometimes I think about which phone Kurt would have opted for. An iPhone? Maybe he would have gone Samsung Galaxy or Huawei. Would he have abstained altogether? Would he be complaining about Twitter on Twitter? What I need to remind myself is that 2021 is a totally different fight to 1994, and maybe sometimes it's okay to 'Breathe the Wave.'©

BANDS

I was in the back of a van with Jacuzzi Boys, a garage rock band from Miami, after a gig. They were dropping me home on their way to a Travelodge. It wasn't a long drive from the venue to Dalston, but spirits were high, and the band were already in their second a capella performance of 'The Lion Sleeps Tonight'. Generally, as mentioned, I have a confused identity, but never do I feel more repressed and British than in the sheer panic of a communal singing session. My mouth opens as if to show willingness, but nothing comes out. My body tenses up, I can feel myself visibly shrinking. With that in mind, I'd asked to be dropped off home so as not to blow my cover as a 'fun guy', under the guise of 'having stuff to do'. Who has stuff to do at 2am other than eat a kebab?

As I screamed my goodbyes over the chorus and slammed the van door shut, I turned to the pavement to see a dealer standing by the closed Tesco Metro, as if expecting me. I had no use for drugs, but it seemed easier to give him my number when approached than explain that I was actually only interested in doner meat. Usually in such a situation I would give the correct number for the first ten digits and then dodge the last one. I can only ever be *just* that dishonest. On this occasion, I was clearly drunk, because as I reached the final number, I paused, froze, and told the truth. My imagination had failed me. I'd forgotten the numbers 2-10. I turned homeward just as the band screeched gleefully on towards Bedford or some equally exotic town.

There's nothing more romantic than the years you spend in a band. A small group of people share a vision and work together, write songs, sacrifice and dream. Your working week is geared around rehearsal. Certain times are out of bounds. The sacrifice feels purposeful. There's a period when being offered £75 for a show as opposed to the usual £50 not only feels like an offer you cannot refuse, but total validation of your life choices thus far. It's consequently always a surprise when one of the members goes on to become Head of Accounts at a regional stationery manufacturer. It's as if they always knew somewhere deep down that being London's second best Trumans Water tribute band wasn't going to be enough.

Buoyed by the fact that Jarvis Cocker had name-dropped the college in the Pulp hit 'Common People', I was convinced I would find my band at Central Saint Martins. I didn't. It turned out everyone wanted to make art. So I did that as well with a liberating sense of detachment, always thinking 'this isn't the thing I'm going to be doing', which in hindsight probably served me well.

Art school taught me how to look, how to expand my thinking, and how to talk about a mushroom for over ten minutes, but everything else I learnt being in a band. This is a sentiment echoed in Richard Phoenix's Rough Trade Books pamphlet *D.I.Y. as Privilege:*

'I was in that band for eight years and I was learning the whole time, whether I knew it or not.'

Being in a band taught me how to work with others, compromise, sell merchandise and string life along on £5 a day. Much to the disappointment of my bandmates, it never taught me how to drive, but they were delighted when I did master how to read a book in the back of a van without throwing up. More than anything, it taught me when to detach myself from work that is personal, and that despite its size, the world can feel quite small when you're bonding over memories of the same grubby dressing room in Sheffield with a band from Miami.

Around my early thirties, it was becoming increasingly difficult to get the four people in my band in the same room at the same time. Relationships were fracturing, the stakes seemed higher, living on the dole was not sustainable, and living off forty compact disc sales (between four of us) was definitely not sustainable either. The band was called Wet Paint, and I'd titled our second album *Woe* because it sounded the same as 'woah'. It was meant to be funny, but it was beginning to play out as an omen.

One day, after the release, while students were rioting in the West End in protest over spending cuts, I was trapped in Oxford Circus's Top Shop, DJing to the empty basement floor to supplement my £5 a day income. An actual gig only paid £50, but you could get £150 in two hours just playing an alphabetised playlist off your laptop in a shop. The only time you could monetise your lack of success was when it was used to legitimise high street band T-shirt knock-offs. Already feeling guilty for allowing myself to be compromised, I picked up Loud And Quiet, the only music paper in which we had a review. Scoring the arts can be so arbitrary, but if it's going to happen, you either want a ten or a one.

Six out of ten.

On the walk home that night, I got a text from an unrecognised number.

'New stuff 10/10'

I couldn't believe it!!! nobody had offered Wet Paint a grain of positivity for our apparently depressing album. My heart sank knowing I didn't recognise the number, and I said as much in an apologetic rendition of 'new phone who dis'.

'Oh my, thank you so much, I can't tell you how much this means to me right now. The timing couldn't have been better, but I'm really embarrassed to say I don't know who this is.'

'We've met loads of times', was the slightly surly reply. I had no idea who I was talking to, but persisting with my questions would come off as rude after this appreciation of my work. A week or so later, they texted back:

'H+C 10/10.'

I eventually worked out these weren't music reviews. It was my friend from the Tesco Metro. He was reviewing his own drugs. I still texted him back to ask if he really meant it when he said the record was a 10/10.

Another thing you learn in a band is strength of character.

AUTHENTICITY

In my foundation year at art college we had a two-week project based around the keyword 'illumination', or one of those words like that. I decided I would make a Christo-like installation. I would bring all the contents of my room to college, arrange them on a table, take a picture of them, then wrap them in a large sheet of canvas and project the image back onto the canvas. I'll give you a moment to recover from having your mind blown.

Only recently did it dawn on me that I never needed to take the three trips on two tubes each way from Finsbury Park to Back Hill with all those boxes of books and pants. I could have just said they were under the canvas. Only I knew the truth. It had never occurred to me that there was an option for it to be any other way. Art was the truth. Art was intention. Art was a problem that didn't exist. Art was the thing nobody asked you to do.

I'd convinced myself that somehow the painful, stressful process of moving house for six hours via public transport would enhance the work. Bear in mind this was 1997. Everything was heavier then. I think this was the first project where I acted on the idea that art was meant to require some level of suffering. Again, I attribute this to Kurt Cobain. My suffering was real, so the art must have had value.

This is in some way true. There is a history of suffering in art. Van Gogh even cut his ear off. 'Suffering for your art' is a phrase people say. Suffering affirms authenticity. It is wired into us when presented with a piece of art that some suffering led to its conception. It adds an allure to the art object in a way which doesn't always translate into everyday life. In years of trying, not one lady has been seduced by my talk of a weird recurring stomach ache.

But as I've since learned, suffering isn't necessarily a requirement. When I discovered a successful artist has a team of assistants helping create their work, it was a shattering blow. The same when I discovered that a comedian's stand-up set was a written work, learned and repeated over and over until it seemed like a natural performance. A comedian did not just stand on a stage and rattle off a perfectly structured two-hour monologue with callbacks and a neat closing line off the top of their head. It was heartbreaking. The same when I saw The Flaming Lips on *The Soft Bulletin* tour on two different nights, and Wayne Coyne said the same 'special' things in between the same songs.

It should have been a relief to know that these works and moments were created by humans who laboured over their craft. That with hard work, such results could be obtainable for myself. That art was not magic. It should not have come as a surprise. Michelangelo had assistants in the 16th century, and he himself

at one point had to make the tea for Ghirlandaio. Maybe once
you reached a certain level of success, your job was to fabricate
authenticity, and you were allowed help to achieve it. At the
end of the day, to the audience, the feeling would be the same.
Maybe everyone was doing a Guns N' Roses—even Nirvana.

Seeking authenticity in art is very much like chasing
your own tail. If you're a dog. Or a man with a tail. A true
authentic voice in the romantic sense would be one that goes
unheard. Art seeks to make connections, but in successfully
doing so, its authenticity is perceived as being cheapened.

In a post-ironic world, what does authenticity mean?
Does it hold any value at all? Are we all too cool for school? Have
we seen everything before? We definitely see a lot, all at the same
time, learning to compartmentalise contrasting emotions on a
five-inch screen. You could be reading a news story about genocide
while being sold a muscle massager. Cindy Sherman, arguably the
creator of the selfie, is now posting selfies on Instagram. When art
is removed from the institutional space of the gallery, what sets it
apart from the rest of the noise? Is there a Duchamp fountain to
be found amongst the content, or is a urinal now just a urinal?

One of the first exhibitions I went to in 1997 at the start
of my foundation course was the Saatchi 'Sensation' show at the
Royal Academy. It may now seem dated in places but having
scraped through the interview process at college with work ghost-
painted by my mum, it was exciting to learn the possibilities of
what art could be. It was controlled anarchy. Art was a carefully
placed kebab, a hospital door, a pickled cow.

The conversation at the time was 'is painting dead?'
It wasn't. Some painters may have died, as people have a tendency
to do, but painting was not dead. The subtext of the question
was 'where is art heading?' Computers were beginning to take
a real foothold in our everyday lives, and the fear for some was
that traditional art forms would be seen as archaic.

One of the artists in the show was Adam Chodzko.
His 'God Look-Alike Contest' featured photos people had sent
in reply to an advert in the back of Loot which said:

'Artist seeks people who think they look like God.'

The work was subtle amongst the more headline-grabbing pieces—the Damien Hirsts, Sarah Lucas' and Tracey Emins, and Marcus Harvey's painting of Myra Hindley.

Here were photos of normal people replying to an advert in a paper. It was genuine, sad, funny and hopeful. It was exciting to me, because this art was once just a classified ad. To my mind, it was as close as I could find to the punk ethos I thought art was supposed to be about. In these pieces, Chodzko's work was out there engaging with the world. It did not wait for the world to come to it. In another work—Flashers (1996-2006)—he recorded one-minute videos onto the unused black tape at the end of rented VHS tapes and returned them to the video shops in the cities he was exhibiting in. I knew I would never find one, but I loved to imagine them out there confusing people falling asleep to the final credits of *Jerry Maguire*.

At the age of 18, I ate these ideas up. I was fortunate enough to have Adam Chodzko as a tutor for a term. At the time, I didn't fully appreciate the influence those works had on me and the work I would go on to make.

Recently, I was in a 'Dog Show'. (A dog-themed art show at Southwark Park Gallery. I don't have a side hustle as a dog, though it's arguable I could pass for one.) The other exhibitors were established names including Martin Creed, David Shrigley, Joan Jonas and Vic Reeves.

Adam Chodzko was exhibiting too. I hadn't seen him in 20 years, and I wanted to tell him that even though I've never really seen those videos, imagining they were out there put me on the path I was meant to go on. I didn't have the guts, though. We were even wearing the same trainers, so I had an in.

The next morning, I discovered I had been burgled. I'm not suggesting he did it, but he definitely left before me. I'm not in a lot of gallery shows, so I did the classy thing and stayed to the end to make sure there was no wine left.

I AM TWIGMAN

In April of 2014, I accidentally stumbled into a project that would clarify for me what differentiates art from the rest of the noise in a world with a permanently ruptured fourth wall: the realisation of an idea versus the idea of an idea.

Everything can be simulated now. We can visually realise anything we want. In *Dawn of the Planet of the Apes* (2014), chimpanzees armed with machine guns are riding horses. It's awesome, but if a chimpanzee armed with a machine gun rode past me on a horse on Kingsland Road, I would shit myself. For art to make an impact, it needs to intersect with real life. Simulations are empty calories.

A good example would be this: when I pitched to write this pamphlet, in my mind it was going to be about the process of getting a billboard installed above the Rio Cinema.

Once I had the mock-up, I felt I had to do it. This is the mock-up.

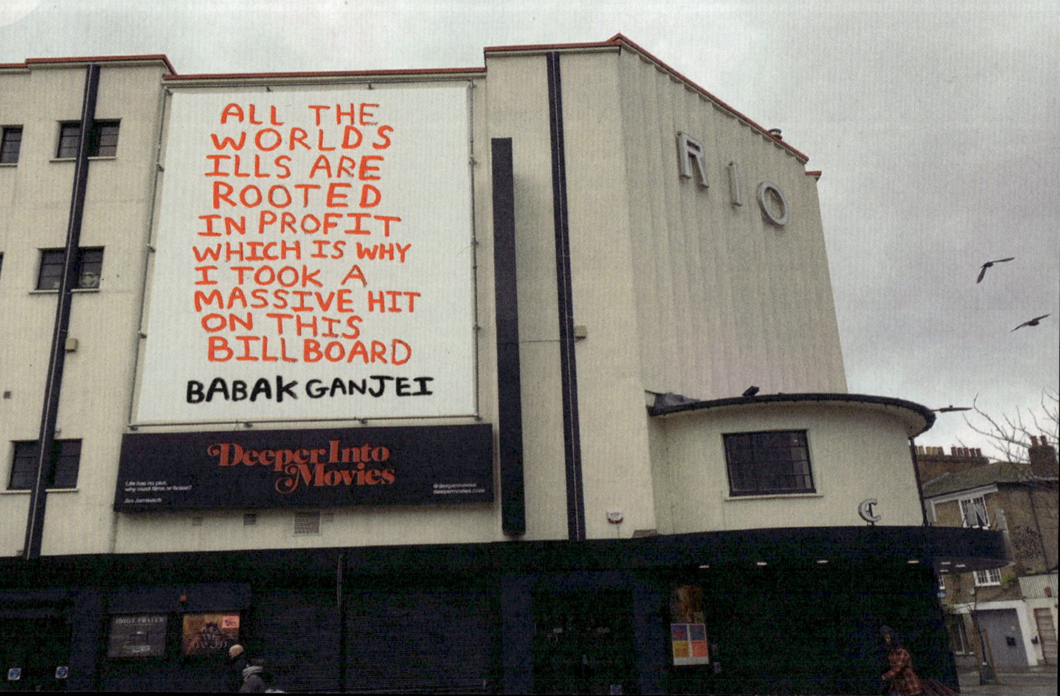

I'd sold some work, and it's important to spend that money on jeopardy. It's not good for an artist to feel too comfortable. If you have made some money, you can afford to make bigger mistakes. I was ready to throw a considerable amount of money at a billboard at the peak of a pandemic. For the solitary walkers. It was funny to me. Sometimes that is enough.

It turned out it was going to cost maybe three times more than I had thought. But now I had the mock-up, and I really wanted to make it happen. I mean, it looks real. I could have posted it on Instagram, basked in a half-hour endorphin rush and saved myself a ton of money. But this is the problem: technology stops reality from happening.

Now the idea has been printed here, and being a cynic, I presume nobody will read these words. They may flick through, see the image, believe I really did it and be mildly impressed. It might serve my ego well, but this picture is not an artwork. To mean anything, the billboard would have to be out on the street, obnoxiously shouting its message. Doing the job of art: causing trouble.

So anyway, on that day in April 2014, I had spent what little money I had on a sandwich I didn't very much enjoy. I was sitting in De Beauvoir Square, a green space in the affluent neighbourhood I had found myself living in, and I really wanted to make back the money I'd spent on the sandwich.

I should add as a caveat that a condition of my making art is that it must be done in the city. This is personal to me. I only feel comfortable living in big cities where the freaks and weirdos are supposed to congregate. I hate the idea of being priced out, and of compromising on what I do. The idea of moving to a cheaper place to make art feels like cheating. The whole game is about surviving. My art is a response to circumstance. For this reason, the city itself can often become a supporting character in the shape things take.

As I sat there with my sandwich wrapper, watching some kids sword fight with sticks, I was reminded of all the twigs my child had asked me to keep in my pockets when he was younger. They were a commodity in the playground. I got up and collected a set of six, all distinct from each other. I went home, photographed them and put them on eBay as Twigs from De Beauvoir Square, giving each one its own identity. The plan was to make back the £4.50 I'd spent in an attempt to go vegetarian (for lunch).

Fundamentally, it was a joke. But it was real. I had measured each twig and recorded its dimensions in the listing. These twigs were a real item. A joke means nothing if it is not based on a truth. I thought it would get a laugh from some friends who would maybe take pity on my situation. I wasn't too proud for pity.

Once a work is put out onto a public forum, it's kind of out of your control what will happen next.

A first bid came through at 99p. Then how I understand it is that either Ed or Ross who booked gigs at the pub I was working at bid on it from the other one's account as a joke when they went to the loo. That evening I took my friend Nikola to see the band Metronomy play at the Brixton Academy. When I left the house, the bidding had reached a hilarious £9.22 after six hours. This was perfect. It was ridiculous, but believable. Also, I was a whole sandwich over my target.

My phone was pinging all throughout the gig with queries from eBay. eBay usernames all being abstract, I dismissed them as friends trying to get in on the joke, but when I got home, I realised the Metro had done a mini article about this bunch of twigs selling for nearly a tenner, and now, over 500 people were watching the auction.

I looked over at the twigs. They had transformed. They were worth £21.35. Sure, there were other twigs out there, but these six I had picked out now had a value placed on them. Suddenly they needed looking after. I put them in a Spongebob tin. They didn't quite fit, but they would be safe in there until the auction was over. They became valuable heirlooms. They became superstars. They essentially got a cordoned-off VIP area in the living room. DO NOT LOOK AT THE TWIGS.

To capitalise on the surge in attention, I began to list a selection of items which either had a fixed value or no determined value at all to see if I could sell them for more. I listed the rights to a TV show idea about a horny monk called Honk.[4] I hand-wrote the lyrics of the theme tune to *The Fresh Prince Of Bel-Air* for £11. I sold an emergency match[5] for £1, and a lucky penny for £1 too. I wasn't exactly raking it in, but the profit margins were impressive—I mean, 9,900% is pretty good. I auctioned a space on my bookshelf as storage. I sold my luck in the form of an unscratched lottery ticket. For the price of a lottery ticket. That was the one I was most fearful would backfire, but it was the sense of risk that made the project work.

I kept my word on all transactions. I wasn't running a business. It was an experiment. There was never any question of not following through on what I was doing.

The morning after the Metro article, I got a call from a producer from Five Live. 'So you're the Twigman,' he said.

I had veered away from ever labelling what I was doing as art, aware that so many stupid stunts are excused that way. I was at the Tate the day somebody defaced a Rothko. I really hoped it was just an accident, and not an artist making a statement. Unfortunately, it was an artist making a statement. It would have arguably been a more powerful statement if it had been an accident. I didn't want the twigs to be contaminated with the negative connotation of art. I wanted to believe, like the people that would stop me in the street for updates on the price, in the total madness of it all.

'So you're the Twigman', the producer repeated. Suddenly, all my pretension was unleashed. I had been working as an artist for almost twenty years, and I did not want to be reduced to being the Twigman. It reminded me of Swampy or something. I instantly visualised a tombstone with 'Twigman' chiselled into it. I was also single and a bit overweight and broke. It didn't feel like this new name would help me.

4 Essentially, I sold a drawing of a monk with an erection for £27. I gave up the rights, so if you ever see the show on Netflix, I am not profiting from that.

5 A box of matches with one match in it.

My lack of enthusiasm on the phone meant I never got a call back to be on whichever show was asking. Who knows how far the twigs could have gone. I let my ego get in the way. I had mistaken the twigs for me, because I am my work.

But I wasn't that bothered. Seven years on, here I am telling you I was the Twigman. If there is a lull at a party, maybe I will whisper it to someone like I'm announcing I'm 'the Man from Milk Tray', and they will say 'I know, you told me at Ben's house yesterday'.

At the time, I was buoyed by articles in different papers pushing things forward. Within twenty-four hours, my joke-turned-art had become top content. Over two thousand people were now following the auction. It was an education in how quickly a small bit of media attention could change everything. Suddenly, eBay was full of twig listings, and some were actually selling. Twigs from Cardiff going for £4, in Birmingham, £5.50. I didn't mind. I couldn't stop people selling twigs. But then I noticed that somebody was selling twigs and using the image from my listing. Now I was angry. Because one thing I knew in all of this was that this seller was not a true artist.

As the week was drawing to a close, the twigs had reached £62. The numbers of people following the auction were increasing, but the bidding had stopped. Pricing your work can always be a tricky issue for an artist with no representation, but what was nice about using eBay was that there was a democratic pricing system. The People would decide what was a reasonable price. And the People seemed to have decided that £62 was reasonable for a set of six twigs from De Beauvoir Square.

Somebody pointed out that I seemed to have a negative review on my page, and I was worried that they were worried that I was going to look like a scammer. I called eBay to find out who had a problem with me. It turned out the man that had bought my unscratched lottery ticket for the cost of a lottery ticket had complained because his item had not been sent. He had not paid the £2, which is why I had not sent it yet. I understood the basics of trade. I emailed this man to ask why he felt the need to complain before paying for the item, and he explained that he thought it was a joke. But he still expected the lottery ticket. I scratched the lottery ticket there and then. I won a MILLION POUNDS!

THE END

If only that was the end.

We hit the day of the sale. I hadn't thought this through, and the auction was ending during my son's swimming lesson, so I sat at the side of the pool refreshing the page, still hoping there would be a final bidding war amongst the 2,500 people watching. There wasn't. £62 was the final price. Still, it was a success. Until the buyer got in touch and said:

'Please tell me this is a joke.'

I tried to explain that a joke is only funny if it actually means something. Without the transaction, all of this was meaningless. If a joke doesn't mean anything, why didn't everybody bid £27,000,000,000? I take comedy very seriously, and it turns out it upsets me greatly when other people don't.

'Why don't you drop it? You got your story.'

She really burst my bubble. I thought I'd created this magic world (this is before Farage and Brexit) where these twigs had been elevated to a superior status. It all hinged on the People understanding the rules, but it turned out not everybody did. I would never force somebody to buy twigs they didn't want, but because I didn't really appreciate the way my project was stomped on and the suggestion that I was just out for a story, I would check in every couple of weeks to see if payment plans had been made. It all got a bit spicy when a 'friend' of the winning bidder took over replies and suggested they would come over with a measuring device and make sure everything was legit. They signed off their reply with:

'It will be good to catch up, buddy.'

Now this sounded mildly threatening. It also suggested they possibly knew me. One day, a friend working in a local pub told me a group had asked if she knew the Twigman. The whole thing was getting a bit *No Country For Old Men*. I never forced the sale, but it was marked as sold, so I ended up paying the commission on it. In the end, I was down £12. It was a bit annoying, because I bet the person using my picture of twigs made a couple of quid.

They didn't get a story, though. And maybe that's the point. There's no story in the picture of a billboard. Maybe I should have spent the money.

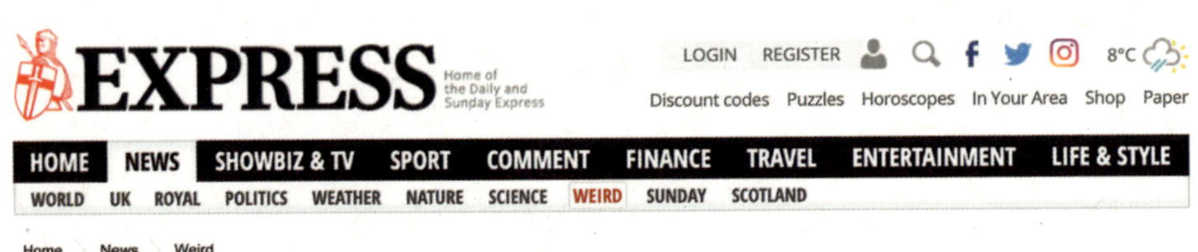

babak ganjei @BabakGanjei · 4m ⌄
@Barclaycard I think you should buy this painting. ebay.co.uk/itm/Babak-Ganj...~
It would be an investment for you, and it would be a massive weight off my shoulders. Is there an Art department to speak to?

Babak Ganjei's Credit Card Painted
ebay.co.uk

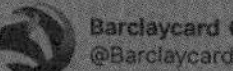

Barclaycard ✓
@Barclaycard

Replying to @BabakGanjei

Hi Babak. We don't actually have a Art department that I can pass this through too. However if you could drop me a DM I'll see if there is anything I can assist you with. Thanks. Dan.

20/01/2018, 16:39

Hi Dan. I'm an artist and I've painted my credit card and it is currently being exhibited in the window of war gallery in London. I think it makes sense if barclaycard buys this painting from me. It's currently on ebay with many people watching the auction. It would be a shrewd investment on your part and at the same time you will get the money back as I will pay it back onto the card. All the best Babak

18:39 ✓

Hi Babak,

I'll pass this on for you, is the card number in the painting your actual Barclaycard number?

Thanks,
Dean.

09:15

Surely it would compromise the integrity of the piece if it wasn't.
All the best
Babak

10:50 ✓

Hi Babak,

I'd recommend we block this card for security reasons, do you want me to block this for you?

Thanks,
Dean.

10:53

Hi Dean,

I'm worried that would compromise the integrity of the piece, I don't know what do you think?

All the best
Babak

Hi Babak,

I understand, I just don't want anyone try to maybe use the card given it shows the card number and expiry date.

Thanks,
Dean

Yesterday 16:12

Thanks Dean

I appreciate the concern, you may be right, I always thought art as in life should be driven by a distinct set of principles, but people seem content with a simulation, I don't exclude myself in this. Or I would not be trying to sell a painting of my debts.
All the best
Babak

10:09 ✓

Hi Babak,

I totally understand but I'm concerned that if anyone uses your card fraudulently then you will be liable for the costs as you've shared your details in such a public way.

If it helps, you don't need to let anyone know that the card isn't a live card. ;-)

Can you confirm that you're OK for me to block it?

Thanks,
Cass

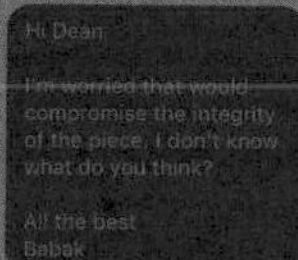

If it's a concern then yes go ahead, you are right people will be happy with the "idea" it's live. It doesn't need to be "real"

Thanks
Babak

Sent ✓

Investment Opportunity (2018)

I tried to get Barclaycard to buy back the debt I had accrued on a credit card.

I painted the card and exhibited it in the window of War Gallery in London, while listing it as a live auction on eBay. It eventually sold for £105. £2200 short.

KEEP UNCOMFORTABLE

I wake up. Before my eyes have adjusted, I grab my phone and check what the awful headline of the day is. The blue light projecting off electronic devices in the dark has somewhat diminished my eyesight, so it takes longer to adjust, allowing for a momentary sense of dread while I wait for confirmation that the world is a turd. Our democracy is compromised. We are living in *The Matrix*. It's all Fake News. We are in one of those kids' books where we can choose the outcome after each chapter, but all the outcomes end in death. It's a heavy first minute.

Then I look out of the window and see a bird in a tree and focus on it for a little while, reminding myself that in the real world (that being the world as seen through the eyes of birds), things are not moving so fast. Hyperbolic rhetoric is replaced with a gentle breeze. There is a man outside holding a ladder, and there is some comfort in knowing that a man still needs a ladder. Before my blood pressure lowers, I refresh the page and look at the news again. Britney Spears is a clone. Now the day can begin.

I put on my shoes.

I'm not going anywhere, but it feels important to be ready to get there as quickly as possible. I refuse to accept anybody having ever made anything of note whilst wearing slippers, a dressing gown, pyjamas or a onesie. I find home clothes depressing. I once went to a friend's house and they were in their home clothes, and it made me feel upset and slightly put off by them, so I made my excuses and left. I feel uncomfortable around people feeling comfortable.

Making art is not supposed to be a pleasurable experience, so it's best to be a little uncomfortable. When a piece is finished, you are allowed the endorphin rush of a job well done, much the

same as finishing a long run. But in both, if you are finding
the process itself pleasurable or therapeutic in some way, you
are doing something wrong and your art is probably bad.

Once fully dressed, I have to speak to someone. Not
email, or text, or send an emoji. I have to have some form of
dialogue with an actual human being. I need to know I am
connected to someone beyond the flat. I say 'dialogue', but
really they just need to be present as I list off some grievances
and observations which have mysteriously accumulated whilst
I was asleep. Some would say this is work for a therapist, but it
is much cheaper and easier to call a friend, and everybody still
has at least one who will pick up a ringing phone.

On the phone to my friend Anna I once said 'life is art,
art is merch'—or that, but the other way round. It was definitely
those words in some order. We both stopped, because it sounded
quite clever. Art is a by-product of experience. As a student, I said
I wanted to get to a point where walking through a Sainsbury's
would be my practice. Luckily, I have my shoes on.

This is how it works. You wake up, you seek the bad
news, you have a conversation, you put on your shoes. Most
of the rest of the day is consumed by trying to avoid eating
the thing you really want to eat (hot dogs).

It's important to have something to drive you
forward. For some, money seems to be that force. Money
is quite cool. It buys you some freedom, which in turn buys
confidence. It's not fair, but that's capitalism. I won't pretend
I am too virtuous for money. I love it when I have it, it's just
never been the driving force.

The driving force for me has always been a fictional
teenage crush. That perpetual ache which will never be resolved.
The long-distance glancing of eyes and the looking away.
It's hard to have this feeling as your *raison d'être* and hold down
a conventional relationship.

I want everyone to like me. And in order to be everyone's,
you must be alone. Some artists will make lots of money and sleep
with everybody, but I'm here to tell you there can be another way.

In the absence of human touch, food becomes the object
of resistance. So we head to the supermarket to flirt and resist.

Not only is the supermarket a great source of tension,
housing a countless number of mistakes and booby traps as it does,
but it is also, for the urban dweller, a theme park, a holiday, and
an escape room (if you happen to get locked in). If you miss green
spaces, go and stand next to some lettuce. If you are the son or
daughter of a farmer missing home, they have eggs of all sizes you
could look at. If you long to be by the sea, ask the person behind
the fish counter if you could stand beside them for a while—just
make sure that you explain you long for the sea.

Supermarkets really are a cultural hub, and some of the
most accessible gallery spaces in the country. They also have hot
dogs—or more accurately, frankfurters. I've come here to avoid
them. I've come here to glance at them from across the aisle and
then look away. I know they are bad for me, but I can't stop.

I have to remind myself of the seven years I had a long-
distance infatuation with a girl in a sheepskin coat wandering
about Bournemouth town centre. For seven years, I said nothing.
When I did finally speak to her—a chance meeting at the
Shepherd's Bush Empire miles and years away from school—
it became apparent she was not the one within three seconds.
She didn't sound like how she had in my head. It turns out
I was in love with her coat.

So, with that in mind, I buy the frankfurters. I haven't
got another seven years to waste glancing at them only to be
disappointed when we finally meet. An artist must embrace the
darkness. Besides, slicing a few into a salad would be considered
almost sophisticated.

My art's primary function is to make good from a mistake.
The sooner a pack of frankfurters is eaten, the sooner art can
be made as an act of atonement. Before you know it, thoughts of
a hot dog salad are by the wayside. Who did I think I was kidding
with such highfalutin notions? Now, in an alleyway metres
from the supermarket, the temptation is too much. There is a
seductive quality in doing the wrong thing, hacking away at the

airtight packaging with my house keys like a psychopath, totally detached from the repercussions of my actions. I know exactly what I am doing, and yet I am in total denial that it is happening. I slide a frankfurter down each sleeve, because instinctively I know it's not a good look to openly eat cold frankfurters from the pack in the street as a man in your forties.

Walking along Upper Street, I know I have hit a new low. The lack of willpower is bewildering. Lifting hand to face and sneaking a bite like Dennis Hopper taking a hit of gas in *Blue Velvet*. Suddenly I'm stopped by a beautiful woman. This will only happen if you have frankfurters up your sleeves. I know this based on the number of times I haven't been recognised without them.

'*Sorry, are you Babak?*'

I confirm this is the case.

'I thought it was you! Sorry to stop you, I just wanted to say I really love your work, it really speaks to me.'

As I nod, lost in her eyes, I wonder if she too has sausage produce sweating under both her sleeves. I also know my day's work is done.

AND ANOTHER THING

I once got asked advice on how to make a real go of it as an artist.

And I told them:

'Make sure you don't have any other skills, then you can't do anything else'.